Tips
AT YOUR
FINGERTIPS:

**Teaching
Strategies for
Adult Literacy
Tutors**

OLA M. BROWN
Editor

INTERNATIONAL
Reading Association
800 Barksdale Road, PO Box 8139
Newark, Delaware 19714-8139, USA

IRA BOARD OF DIRECTORS

The International Reading Association attempts, through its publications, to provide a forum for a wide spectrum of opinions on reading. This policy permits divergent viewpoints without implying the endorsement of the Association.

Director of Publications   Joan M. Irwin
Assistant Director of Publications   Wendy Lapham Russ
Associate Editor   Christian A. Kempers
    Matthew W. Baker
Assistant Editor   Janet Parrack
Production Department Manager   Iona Sauscermen
Graphic Design Coordinator   Boni Nash
Design Consultant   Larry Husfelt
Desktop Publishing Supervisor   Wendy Mazur
Desktop Publishing   Anette Schütz-Ruff
    Cheryl Strum
Production Services Editor   David Roberts

Photo Credits   Laima Druskis Photography, pp. 5, 19, 35, 79; CLEO Freelance Photo, p. 61; Image Productions ©1991 by Jeffrey High, p. 97

Library of Congress Cataloging in Publication Data

   Tips at your fingertips: teaching strategies for adult literacy tutors/Ola M. Brown, editor
      p.   cm.
      Includes bibliographical references and index.
      1. Reading (Adult education).   2. English language—Rhetoric—Study and teaching. 3. Tutors and tutoring.   4. Elementary education of adults.   I. Brown, Ola M.
   LC5225.R4T56   1996
   374'.012'0973—dc20   95-43785
   ISBN 0-87207-141-3 (pbk.)

CONTENTS

Introduction

This book was developed because of a need for tutors in the Atlanta (Georgia) BellSouth Literacy Project to have an instructional resource to use with adults at various levels of learning. At the request of Bill Hammond (State Department Liaison for the Georgia Council of the International Reading Association), the state reading association under the presidency of Janet Busboom agreed to make a contribution to this worthwhile project. At the conclusion of the GCIRA's Annual Reading Conference in March 1994, I was appointed by Janet Busboom to coordinate this effort. When I completed this endeavor, it was determined that perhaps other literacy programs and tutors could benefit by the availability and use of such a resource. The purpose of this book, therefore, is to provide a compilation of research-based or "tried and tested" strategies adapted for use by literacy providers who often have limited time and resources and who tutor small groups of adult students or in one-on-one situations.

I have taught middle, secondary, and adult reading classes in my role as a college instructor, and I currently serve as a part-time learning facilitator for Levi Strauss and Company's employee literacy program in Valdosta, Georgia.

I have always been keenly aware of the International Reading Association's *Journal of Reading* as a fundamental teaching resource, and I use it extensively. Consequently, I decided to adapt strategies from the articles in the *Journal of Reading* for this book. I also agree with the numerous researchers who contend that learning is best facilitated through holistic instruction, which involves the integration of the language arts—listening, writing, speaking, and reading—as opposed to isolated skill instruction. This finding holds true for learning at all levels—especially for adult learners whose wide array of experiences make holistic instruction both logical and meaningful. Thus, I selected *JR* articles based on this philosophy.

The *JR* articles I have adapted span 14 years, from 1980 to 1994. In addition to articles that describe strategies that were designed for and used with adults, I have adapted articles containing certain strategies that worked well with other age levels and seemed promising for adult students. These strategies have been used with adult students and are interspersed throughout the sections of this book.

This book is divided into six sections, although many of the strategies overlap among these sections. Section I consists of ideas and strategies that can help tutors and program coordinators develop an effective core curriculum for adults that includes whole language, integrated language arts, language experience, and modified Reading Recovery intervention. Section II contains general information and strategies regarding adult instruction. Section III comprises various strategies for improving reading comprehension, including comprehension monitoring, following directions, inferring main idea, using the schema theory and cooperative learning, paired storytelling, and critical reading. Section IV includes numerous writing strategies such as letter writing, journal writing, creative writing, and précis writing. Section V stresses vocabulary development using such strategies as structured overviews, context clues, and word banks. Section VI details strategies that use alternative reading materials including picture books, magazines, classic novels, tabloids, and annual reports. Finally, the appendixes provide additional information that is useful to adult literacy teachers and tutors.

I would like to acknowledge and express my deepest gratitude to adult literacy students at Levi Strauss and Company in Valdosta who successfully performed many of the strategies that are included in this book. Special thanks are also in order for three wonderful persons, Carolyn Shaw (Valdosta State University) and Betty Gulley and Mona Gibbs (Levi Strauss and Company), for typing portions of the manuscript. Finally, I am deeply appreciative to Chris Kempers, Associate Editor at the International Reading Association, for her expertise in editing the manuscript and providing the finishing touch.

It is my sincere hope that as literacy providers you will find this handbook to be a valuable instructional tool and that it will, indeed, provide "tips at your fingertips."

SECTION I

Developing an Effective
Adult Literacy Curriculum

Applying the Whole Language Theory to Adult Literacy Programs
from "Teaching Adult New Readers the Whole Language Way"
by Donald Keefe & Valerie Meyer

Using the Language Experiences of Adults in Literacy Programs
from "Guidelines and a Holistic Method for Adult Basic Reading
Programs" by Gary M. Padak & Nancy D. Padak

Using Oral Histories and Writing in an Adult Basic Skills Program
from "Writing Our Lives: An Adult Basic Skills Program"
by Bird B. Stasz, Roger G. Schwartz, & Jared C. Weeden

**Integrated Language Arts for English as a Second Language
Students**
from "Working with New ESL Students in a Junior High School
Reading Class" by Beth M. Arthur

An Intervention Program for Adult Literacy Students

from "Reading Rescue: Intervention for a Student 'At Promise'"
by Nancy G. Lee & Judith C. Neal

Applying the Whole Language Theory to Adult Literacy Programs

The article "Teaching Adult New Readers the Whole Language Way" by Donald Keefe and Valerie Meyer, from the November 1991 issue of *Journal of Reading*, offers ways to apply the whole language philosophy in adult education settings. The authors contend that using strategies based on whole language methods may help adult literacy programs become more effective. This adaptation summarizes the tenets of whole language theory and Brian Cambourne's (1988) conditions for holistic literacy learning, which the authors of the article expand on to form a basis for a whole language approach to adult literacy instruction.

The whole language theory supports the following principles:

- The language arts—reading, writing, speaking, and listening—should be taught in an integrated fashion.
- Language skills such as spelling, grammar, punctuation, and capitalization are enhanced through the integration of the language arts.
- Language usage should make sense to the reader.
- Language is learned through practice; therefore, reading, writing, speaking, and listening should be done often.

7

The following seven conditions for holistic literacy learning (Cambourne, 1988) are essential to whole language. They are explained in terms of their application to the adult literacy curriculum:

- Immersion. Whole, relevant, functional, and meaningful written language should be an integral part of instruction. This includes environmental and logo print, stories in which the text follows a highly predictable pattern, repeated readings, language experience stories (real-life stories that are dictated by the student), and read-alouds.

- Demonstration. As stories are used in instruction, you should demonstrate how print works. These demonstrations should emphasize reading and writing left to right and top to bottom, distinguishing between letters and words, sounding out parts of words, using periods and capital letters, and sequencing ideas.

- Engagement. Students should be involved in the demonstrations so that learning will result. Becoming engaged and paying attention are most important.

- Expectations. Build self-confidence in students by letting them know that you care. Make them aware of their accomplishments—no matter how small—and encourage them to continue practicing their reading and writing skills.

- Responsibility. Adult students must take responsibility for their own learning. They must provide input regarding what is important and interesting to them, as well as goals that they have for themselves.

- Approximation. Adult students' approximations or guesses should be expected and accepted rather than quickly corrected. They must be allowed to take risks and make mistakes as natural steps toward learning.

- <u>Employment</u>. Students must be given opportunities to use reading and writing in a functional way. For example, being able to read the directions on a garment label and write a message for someone are important applications of literacy.

- <u>Response</u>. Students should be taught reading and writing in the context of their own attempts or responses to read and write. Avoid emphasizing word lists, grammar lessons, and phonics skills that are separate from actual attempts to read or write. Supportive feedback should be given to students in response to a task completed.

Reference
Cambourne, B. (1988). *The whole story: Natural learning and the acquisition of literacy in the classroom.* Richmond Hill, Ont.: Scholastic-TAB.

Using the Language Experiences of Adults in Literacy Programs

Programs for adult literacy learners should offer theory-based instruction that focuses on learner needs. In an article published in the March 1987 issue of *Journal of Reading*, Gary M. Padak and Nancy D. Padak discuss some guidelines that can form the foundation for an effective adult reading curriculum. In "Guidelines and a Holistic Method for Adult Basic Reading Programs" the authors also describe whole language instructional strategies that they

9

have found successful. Here, in this adaptation of the article, these guidelines are highlighted, and some ideas are given for providing a supportive environment for growth in reading using the language experience approach—a strategy based on students' dictated material. This approach uses learners' oral language and life experiences.

Guidelines for an Adult Literacy Curriculum

- Instruction should be focused on the adults' experiences, interests, and needs or goals.
- Instruction should emphasize reading as an active search for meaning in print. Meaning-based instruction incorporates reading, writing, speaking, and listening.
- Instruction should address the affective, or emotional, needs of the learners in order for them to become lifelong, independent readers.

Language Experience Strategy

1. Have the learner retell some event in which he or she has participated to initiate a dictation. Options for this step may include the following:

   - Encourage the learner to do a dictated autobiography that might include recollections of memorable events in his or her life. This could be accomplished by having the learner do several dictations as described in Step 1 and compiling these accounts. Students will also learn about the elements of a book, which include the contents page and title page. Photographs can be included in the finished product to make this project a valuable instructional tool.

- Engage in discussions about local or national current events or read aloud recent news articles to trigger dictations. This activity can encourage students to read newspapers and news magazines.

- Have the learner talk about a certain hobby or interest. Dictation should follow that focuses on what the learner already knows about the subject. Try to obtain printed material on the subject to read aloud to the learner or place on audiotapes for listening. This new information can result in another dictation by the learner.

- Provide the learner with everyday print material that will initiate conversation. Materials such as telephone directories, maps, and advertisements contain numerous possibilities for generating language.

- Have the learner dictate a letter to a business concerning merchandise purchased, to an insurance agency regarding a claim, or to an employer announcing resignation.

2. Record all dictated accounts word for word. Once written, the accounts should be read back for the learner to make any changes. These accounts can then be used to introduce language mechanics such as punctuation and capitalization and many other aspects of language. The learner will retain the information better if he or she discovers the language aspects without direct instruction.

Using Oral Histories and Writing in an Adult Basic Skills Program

In the September 1991 issue of *Journal of Reading* Bird B. Stasz, Roger G. Schwartz, and Jared C. Weeden describe an adult basic skills program that promotes empowerment and ownership. In their article "Writing Our lives: An Adult Basic Skills Program," they combine the whole language philosophy with the writing process and oral history strategies. This approach allows adults to demonstrate their strengths and learn from their weaknesses because the process depends on information about their own lives. This gives students ownership of their learning, which in turn empowers them as learners. The program is a class run by the Student Literacy Corps, which places trained college student volunteers with Head Start mothers in an effort to raise their literacy levels, so they are better equipped to help their children. An adaptation of the program implementation steps follows.

1. Establish rapport with adult students through general conversation.
2. Engage students in a meaningful writing process of recollecting, discussing, writing, and rewriting. Using this technique students can recapture the events of their lives that they love best.
3. Ask students to recollect pleasant events of their childhood or any event that had some effect on their lives. Encourage them to use all their senses to help them recall.

4. Allow students the flexibility of exploring their own world and capturing the spirit and language of their world in print. Record each idea until the list covers the page. Ask questions to elicit additional responses.

5. Decide with students which ideas are important. Organize these ideas into paragraphs.

6. Work with students on developing paragraphs, emphasizing main ideas, and supporting details.

7. Share the work of adult students by binding together a collection of completed narratives for others to read.

Integrated Language Arts for English as a Second Language Students

Strategies for using an integrated language arts program, as described in Beth M. Arthur's article "Working with New ESL Students in a Junior High School Reading Class," are adapted in the following list, which is divided into three areas: writing, reading and listening, and speaking. In her article, published in the May 1991 issue of *Journal of Reading*, Arthur stresses that she used the same whole language program—immersing her students in all the language arts—with her junior high school ESL students as she did with beginning English-speaking readers. These strategies can also be adapted well into an adult literacy curriculum.

Writing

Using Communication Logs

Have students use notebooks or composition paper with lines and construction paper for front and back covers. Make the first entry in the log, stating the purpose—to get to know your students better—and including questions that can be easily read and answered. Encourage students to ask questions in their written responses. Students are free to use other resources such as dictionaries and bilingual persons in the home to help with these responses in the logs.

Working with Computers

Look for computer programs that allow students to create conversation for people or characters to go into blank conversational balloons, such as cartoons in which the characters do not have speech. Promote writing by using these programs with students who are interested in working with computers or animation.

Using Wordless Stories or Books

Have students write stories to accompany the pictures. After editing the stories (with students' input), have the students copy them into a book.

Reading and Listening

Reading Predictable Books

Read books with predictable text patterns aloud, and record the readings on tape. Allow students to read along independently with the tapes from the books. Focus on literal and inferential comprehension as well as figurative language as you discuss the books with the students.

Using Commercially Prepared Books on Tape

As students gain proficiency with predictable book tapes, offer them more difficult commercially prepared books on tape. Try to locate sets of books with cassettes that contain simple language, limited text, but meaningful concepts for repeated listening (for example, Bill Martin's science book series on nature, woodland, and seashore).

Speaking

Talking about Everyday Items

Engage students in conversation prompted by pictures of everyday items such as the ones found in some picture books, catalogs, magazines, and newspaper advertisements. Clip items from ads and place them on index cards along with the word naming the pictures so students can practice saying the words. ESL students can also write their language's equivalent on the cards. Creating word banks, a strategy described in Section V of this handbook, is an outgrowth of this activity.

Using the Language Experience Approach

Use the language experience approach, explained in the strategy earlier in this section, and modifications of it to promote language-related activities with ESL students. Through sharing experiences, students are able to further develop their oral language and speech skills.

An Intervention Program for Adult Literacy Students

In the article "Reading Rescue: Intervention for a Student 'At Promise'," which appeared in the December 1992 issue of *Journal of Reading*, authors Nancy G. Lee and Judith C. Neal present a case study about David—a middle school student who might have been labeled "at risk" because of his low level of reading achievement. But, because David had no physical or emotional factors that were influencing his poor reading achievement, the authors surmised he was "at promise" and able to make progress in his reading performance. Here is a brief outline of the one-on-one intervention program that the authors used with David after they conducted a multifaceted assessment to determine David's specific reading capabilities. This program is an adaptation of Marie Clay's 1985 instructional intervention model, which is intended for first graders but can easily be applied to adult literacy students.

1. Read familiar material. Have the student select material from chapter books or language experience stories to reread for building confidence and fluency.
2. Read aloud to the student. Continue to read new material to the student (material that was started at the end of the previous session). This is a time to demonstrate regular breathing during

reading and appropriate expression to fit the meaning. Also, this added component of the lesson helps promote an appreciation for reading as an enjoyable activity.

3. Take a running record on part of the new material used in the previous session. In this procedure the student reads aloud a selected portion of material while you note any discrepancies between print and pronunciation. Mark each word pronounced accurately with a check; indicate mispronunciation by writing the word that is said above the printed word. Also indicate successful self-corrections by the student by placing a "c" over the corrected words. By taking a running record during each session, you can establish a focus for the next component of the intervention.

4. Work with words and letters. Using a magnetic board and plastic letters, typical activities include identifying word parts, developing awareness of sounds in words, examining similarly spelled words, and developing various strategies for pronouncing unfamiliar words.

5. Write through a language experience. (See the strategy "Using the Language Experiences of Adults in Literacy Programs" earlier in this section for more details about this approach.) Using a computer and word processing software, have the student dictate a brief story, while you type what he or she says. Have the student dictate stories about events in his or her life in order to create materials that are easy to read. In subsequent sessions, the student can reread and edit these stories.

6. Read new material. As you introduce new material for the student to read, scan it for unfamiliar words and concepts. Read part of the new material to the student. Then, have the student repeat the same text aloud with you (paired unison reading). This is a way to practice reading for fluency and mastery. In the next session, take a running record using this material.

17

Comments and Notes:

SECTION II

General Tips and Instructional Strategies

Assessing the Adult Beginning Reader
from "Exploring Reading with Adult Beginning Readers"
by Nancy D. Padak, Jane L. Davidson, & Gary M. Padak

General Tips for Adult Literacy Tutors
from "Lingering Feelings of Failure: An Adult Student Who Didn't
Learn to Read" by Valerie Meyer

General Literacy Strategies to Use with Adult New Readers
from "Case Study—Norman: Literate at Age 44" by Valerie Meyer,
Sharon L. Estes, Valorie K. Harris, & David M. Daniels

Teaching Reading as Meaning Making
from "Learning to Read and Write at 26" by Anne D. Forester

How to Choose a Good Fiction Book
from "How to Choose a Good Book" by Hilda E. Ollmann

Assessing the Adult Beginning Reader

For literacy teachers and tutors to meet the challenge of helping adult learners become competent, avid readers, they must first understand these adults as readers. Many times formal or standardized testing is used to obtain information about reading ability; however, this method has been found to have limitations for instructional planning. Nancy D. Padak, Jane L. Davidson, and Gary M. Padak explain several alternative strategies for exploring beginning adult readers' perceptions about their reading and reading abilities in the article "Exploring Reading with Adult Beginning Readers" from the September 1990 issue of *Journal of Reading*. This list briefly summarizes these alternatives to standardized testing to help determine strengths and weaknesses of students. Based on information collected during this ongoing process of assessment, you can make decisions about what type of instruction your adult students need.

Discovering Students' Ideas about Reading

In individual interviews, ask about the students' background, interests, and goals. Also inquire about their thoughts on readers, reading, and reading strategies. Sample interview questions follow.

Background, Interests, and Goals

Where do you and your family live?

What types of jobs have you had?

What are your interests?

How do you spend your spare time?

How did you become interested in this program?

What are your short- and long-term goals?

Ideas about Reading

Who do you wish you could read like?

How well does this person read?

What is reading?

What should good readers do?

Are you a good reader? Why or why not?

How does someone become a better reader?

Awareness of Reading Strategies

What do you do if you do not know a word?

What happens if you are not able to figure out the word?

How do you remember something that you've read?

Are you able to remember what you read?

Do you understand everything that you read? If not, what do you do?

Assessing Learners' Comprehension Ability

The Directed Listening-Thinking Activity (DL-TA) Strategy (Davidson, Padak, & Padak, 1989)

1. Choose a text that is unfamiliar to the students.

2. Ask the students to make predictions about the text content and to provide reasons for their ideas.

3. Read a portion of the text and ask the listeners to evaluate their predictions.

4. Have the students predict what might be presented next and why they think so. Discussions should center on the questions "What do you think?" and "Why do you think so?"

The Retelling Strategy

1. Have students listen to an unfamiliar text, and then let them tell everything they remember about what was read.

2. After an initial retelling, provide prompts to encourage further response without giving clues.

3. Write extensive notes or make a tape recording of the retelling for assessment. In analyzing the retelling, listen for the presence of main ideas and significant supporting details.

Exploring Students' Knowledge of Words

The following steps use dictation as a diagnostic tool.

1. Engage students in a discussion about a topic.

2. Ask students to summarize the discussion.

3. Write each statement exactly as it is spoken, using standard spelling, capitalization, and punctuation.

4. Ask the students to read the information aloud and take note of the ease, fluency, and correctness of words pronounced.

5. Have the students read the dictation again silently and underline all the known words. Complete this process twice.

6. Ask the students to identify each underlined word.

Through this process, you can determine a student's ability to learn new words in familiar context. You also can make note of a student's word-identification strategies with a dictation. For example, you can determine whether a student tries to employ context clues or phonics.

Reference

Davidson, J.L., Padak, N.D., & Padak, G.M. (1989). *Reading, writing, thinking for life* (Teachers' manual, level 1, set 1). Monroe, NY: Trillium.

General Tips for Adult Literacy Tutors

This list of general tips for adult literacy tutors is adapted from the article "Lingering Feelings of Failure: An Adult Student Who Didn't Learn to Read," by Valerie Meyer, originally published in the December 1987 issue of *Journal of Reading*. The "lingering feelings of failure" in the article's title refer to Meyer's sense of having failed a student who had come to her at a stage in her professional life when she was not prepared to face the unique challenges posed by an adult learner. At the time this article was written, Meyer had gained the knowledge she needed, but it was too late for the student she failed to help. This list reflects her growth as a reading educator and offers practical advice to all who try—and sometimes fail—to help adults learn to read.

- Spend time getting to know your students. Discovering what they like to do will provide a springboard for teaching reading and writing. Oral language skills also can be assessed through conversations with the students.

- Help your students see themselves as readers. Show them that reading environmental print (such as food product boxes, street signs, and store names) is a type of reading.

- Read aloud information of interest to the adults you tutor. This will provide valuable background information as well as improve their receptive language skills.

- Be sure that your students have interesting reading material at home. If possible, meet them at the local library, help them obtain a library card, and guide them in the selection of books.

- Prepare audiotapes of some articles, stories, or poems for your students to practice reading. Reading along with the tapes will help relieve some anxiety and ensure a successful activity.

- Place the responsibility for learning in the hands of the learners. Impress upon them the need to practice reading every day.

- Make reading a realistic experience for your adult students using concrete activities and materials that have meaning for them. Provide them with several practical materials to read such as newspapers, magazines, menus, television schedules, application forms, and so forth.

- Set realistic, short-term goals with the students so that accomplishments may be realized and reached.

General Literacy Strategies to Use with Adult New Readers

In their article "Case Study—Norman: Literate at Age 44," from the September 1991 issue of *Journal of Reading,* authors Valerie Meyer, Sharon L. Estes, Valorie K. Harris, and David M. Daniels present the extraordinary story of Norman, a man whose determination to learn to read inspired everyone around him. This list of general strategies, adapted from the article, demonstrates adult literacy instruction that is purposeful and that looks at learning from a holistic viewpoint, stressing the integration of all literacy skills. Norman was successful because his tutors provided him with support and encouragement, and they gave him opportunities to see the wonderful progress his hard work produced.

Creating an Environmental Print Book

1. Have students flip through magazines and cut out advertisements for products that are identifiable.
2. Tape ads to blank paper and write the product's name or a description of it next to each ad.
3. Have students continue doing Steps 1 and 2 at home. The outcome will be a large environmental print book with which a sight vocabulary (words that are immediately recognizable) can be built.

4. Drop the pictures and transfer the words to flashcards. In this way, a word bank can be created for additional study and review. (Word banks are described in the "Increasing Vocabulary" section of this handbook.)

Using Language Experience Stories

1. Introduce language experience stories to the students. These are stories told by the students about things that are familiar. (The language experience approach is explained in detail in Section I.)

2. As the students relate the information, write it on paper for further use.

3. Have students practice reading the stories that have been dictated. Because the words in the stories are given by the students, they are easy for them to recognize and remember.

Practicing Writing

1. Ask students to copy short, interesting passages.

2. Have students write in a daily journal about life experiences (past or present).

3. Have students complete simple sentences. Use predictable and repetitious sentences such as, "I like my _____, but I don't like _____" or "I like _____ in my coffee, but my co-worker doesn't like _____ in his coffee."

Other Strategies to Promote Literacy

• Find an interesting story to read aloud about an adult who achieved success by working hard and continuously.

• Provide students with role models of reading and writing.

- Provide a variety of reading materials from which students may select. Allow them the opportunity to discover known words in print.

- Include in each tutoring session a selection to be read to students and one to be read with them (alternating reading). Also, include a writing activity and an independent reading activity.

- Encourage students to skip unknown words and use context clues to figure out the words. Help them become risk takers.

- Encourage students to make predictions before reading and then read to determine if predictions were correct.

- Refrain from having students memorize vocabulary words from a sight-word list, having them work page by page in a workbook, or having them do isolated skill sheets.

Teaching Reading as Meaning Making

When learners are encouraged to rely on their own knowledge of language and learning strategies, they are able to make progress in their literacy learning. In her article "Learning to Read and Write at 26," which appeared in the April 1988 issue of *Journal of Reading*, Anne D. Forester outlines what she calls the "literacy continuum": stages of oral language development, spelling/printing, writing/ composing, and reading. By showing this continuum, Forester draws parallels between the need for both young and mature learners to generate their own spelling and with it a knowledge of letters and their sounds. She discusses the progress of her adult student, Laura, through this continuum and points out that her progress is due mainly to Laura's moving through the stages of spelling development—beginning to invent spelling and compose messages—much as young learners do.

This list of strategies, adapted from Forester's article, emphasizes that tutors should encourage students to use their own experience to aid reading, which reinforces the idea that the students *do* have resources to draw on for literacy learning.

- Help students realize how familiar they are with environmental print such as product labels, traffic signs, store names, street names, and so forth.
- Use conversation and discussion to link sight-word vocabulary with student interests.
- Encourage students to work in pairs or in small groups based on common interests.
- Model fluent reading of a variety of materials such as poetry, directions, interesting news articles, short stories, and so on.
- Encourage students to follow along as you read aloud in one-on-one sessions.
- Produce tapes of books for students to use and read along with.
- Create modified cloze materials (text that has words omitted in order to measure a person's ability to restore those words) by block-

ing out the most predictable words first and shifting to more difficult ones later.

- Discuss with students their reasons for wanting to learn to read.

- Invite students to bring in materials of their choice for practice reading.

- Let the students find their own comfortable level of reading. Encourage them to read widely.

How to Choose a Good Fiction Book

This adaptation of the article "How to Choose a Good Book," from the Open to Suggestion department in the April 1993 issue of *Journal of Reading*, outlines Hilda E. Ollmann's strategies for helping students select literature. Ollmann presents a seven-step "strategy sheet" that directs students to record clues about a potential book choice and then make predictions about the book's content and style. Ollmann has found that this strategy makes students really think about their selections, and they have better luck finding a book they enjoy.

Introduce the strategy sheet for choosing a good book, which is on page 32, by modeling it in front of the group. Provide each student with the seven-step strategy sheet and have them record clues about a potential book choice in the lefthand column of their sheet. From this information predictions can be made about the content, style, and interest of the book in the righthand column. The following numbered steps correspond to the numbers on the strategy sheet.

1. Ask students to examine the title. Tell them to list the title in the lefthand column of the strategy sheet. Ask students to write their predictions about what the story might be about, considering the title, in the righthand column.

2. Tell the students to look at the pictures or illustrations in the book. In the lefthand column, direct them to list the illustrations or describe them. Then, based on the illustrations, they can predict more about the content of the book in the righthand column.

3. Have students read about the author of the book from the book jacket and discuss his or her other writings in small groups. Make predictions in the righthand column, based on the author's life and writing style in other books, about what this particular book might be like.

4. Direct students to quote important phrases from the book jacket or backcover summary in the lefthand column and predict the probable storyline and mood in the righthand column.

5. Ask students to read the first page of the book. In the righthand column, direct students to guess a bit more about the storyline and mood of the book.

6. Again, repeat Step 5 with a randomly selected page two-thirds of the way into the book.

7. Ask the students to write any remaining ideas about the book and come to a conclusion or decision about reading the book.

After completing a strategy sheet two or three times, students usually can follow the steps mentally and have no need to write them down.

Strategy Sheet for Choosing a Fiction Book

Strategy Notes	My Prediction
1. Title	1.
2. Illustrations	2.
3. Author	3.
4. Book jacket summary	4.
5. First page	5.
6. A page two-thirds into the book	6.

7. My conclusion

Note: This strategy sheet was adapted by Hilda E. Ollmann from the format of a dialectical journal [see Berthoff, A.E. (1987). Dialectical notebooks and the audit of meaning. In T. Fulwiler (Ed.), *The journal book*. Upper Montclair, NJ: Boynton/Cook].

Comments and Notes:

SECTION III

Improving Reading Comprehension

Comprehension Monitoring: Recommended Strategies
from "Comprehension Monitoring: Definition and Practice"
by Murray M. Pitts

Comprehending and Following Written Directions
from "How to Develop Independence in Following Written Directions"
by William A. Henk & John P. Helfeldt

Schema Theory and Cooperative Learning
from "Schema Activation, Cooperation, and Adult Literacy Instruction"
by Dolores Perin

Inferring Main Ideas from Text
from "Processing Main Ideas Through Parallel Lesson Transfer"
by David W. Moore & John E. Readence

Comprehension Monitoring: Recommended Strategies

The following list of comprehension-monitoring strategies and ideas about how to teach them to students is adapted from Murray M. Pitts's article "Comprehension Monitoring: Definition and Practice," published in the March 1983 issue of *Journal of Reading*. In his article, Pitts presents a brief overview of current theories and research related to comprehension monitoring—the ability to judge the quality of one's understanding—and offers suggestions for teaching comprehension-monitoring strategies. He emphasizes that "A total instructional program in comprehension monitoring should include familiarizing students with common comprehension obstacles, teaching them to question their comprehension, and instructing them in remedial actions when they fail to comprehend text."

General Comprehension-Monitoring Strategies

- Ignore and read on if unknown information is not critical to understanding.
- Change the rate of reading if some of the pertinent information is missed by reading too fast.
- Suspend judgment if reading more slowly does not lead to understanding.

37

• Form a tentative hypothesis if suspending judgment does not lead to clarification.

• Reread if too many possible interpretations can be seen.

• Go to an expert source if all fails.

A Three-Stage Modeling Method for Teaching Students Comprehension-Monitoring Strategies

1. <u>Modeling stage</u>. Read an unfamiliar passage aloud to the class, ask relevant questions, and describe the monitoring strategies to be used.

2. <u>Student participation stage</u>. Ask students to formulate questions, note confusions, make educated guesses, find supporting evidence, and suggest strategies for correction.

3. <u>Read silently stage</u>. Have students do their own monitoring while you stand by to suggest strategies when reading difficulties arise.

Comprehending and Following Written Directions

It is important for all students to be able to comprehend procedural text. William A. Henk and John P. Helfeldt, in their article "How to Develop Independence in Following Written Directions," which appeared in the April 1987 issue of *Journal of Reading*, explain why simple written directions often present a problem for readers of all levels. They also contend that direction-following skills can be learned through a series of instructional activities. The steps involved in these activities—awareness, modeling, guided practice, and independent practice—are outlined in the following adaptation of this article.

Awareness

To help students discover what skills are being learned and why, when, and how to use them, discuss with your class the general instances when written directions must be followed. Try to help students develop an awareness of the skills necessary for certain types of directions, such as the need for physical ability to repair an object. Also, point out that drawings are often included with some directions for construction of items.

Modeling

Show and explain how to finish a task or use a skill by using a "think-aloud" procedure—walking students through each thought and step:

1. Direct students to survey any illustrations to get a general idea of the scope of the task and of what the finished product should look like.

2. Have students read all the instructions once. Then, they should read each step cautiously and match it with the corresponding illustration. Encourage them to visualize themselves completing each step.

3. Have students read for a third time to help commit the overall plan to mind.

4. Direct the students to actually perform the task, looking back to the text and illustrations as needed.

Guided Practice

Focus students' attention on important elements of written directions by having them look for and highlight verbs, location cues, sequence cues, and unfamiliar words. For example, in the directions "First close the lefthand door, then shut the bay window" the action words students should pay attention to are *close* and *shut*; the location for the door is *lefthand*; the sequence is indicated by the words *first* and *then*; and the unfamiliar word may be *bay*. The following activities that stress the importance of these cues can be used with small groups or individuals:

• Place each step of a set of directions on a separate index card. Mix the cards and have students place them in correct order, identifying the cues used.

• Place illustrations and written directions on separate sets of cards. Shuffle both sets and have learners match written directions with the illustrations, justifying their choices.

• Have students follow directions using illustrations only. Then ask them to write their own set of directions to match the illustrations. Discuss any problems in the written versions and make the corrections.

• Omit a key word or a whole step and see if students can supply the missing information in the blank space and then describe their reasoning.

• Change a part of the directions, and then have students discover the problem caused by the change.

- Have students bring in actual directions related to work at home that are difficult to follow as written. Let them rewrite the directions for greater clarity.

Independent Practice

Allow students to follow several sets of directions on their own, going from the less difficult to the more complex directions. This extensive practice should result in some transfer of ability in following directions in materials beyond the classroom.

Schema Theory and Cooperative Learning

One challenge for an adult literacy instructor is to maintain motivation among students. It has been found that adult students' knowledge of the world and their active participation in learning are two conditions that are very important for keeping students interested in academic tasks. In her article "Schema Activation, Cooperation, and Adult Literacy Instruction," which was published in the October 1988 issue of *Journal of Reading*, Dolores Perin explains an activity for teaching reading comprehension that uses these conditions based on the schema theory in reading and cooperative learning. Schema theory holds that teachers should activate students' familiarity and interest prior to an academic task; cooperative learning promotes using tasks in which students need to cooperate, combined with incentives based on the performance of the cooperating groups. This adaptation outlines the steps in Perin's reading comprehension activity.

1. Select a text to be used for reading comprehension that is consistent with student knowledge and interest.

2. Divide the class into small, heterogeneous groups.

3. Appoint an individual in each group to be the recorder and leader. These individuals should be those who would not otherwise volunteer.

4. Before passing out the text, write a word or phrase on the chalkboard from the selected text that represents a concept and is familiar to students.

5. Have the groups write as many words or phrases as they know that relate to the word on the board.

6. Have the groups repeat Step 5 using another word or phrase you write on the board.

7. Write a statement on the board that represents an interesting main idea from the text. Ask the groups to discuss and determine whether they agree with the statement based on their own experiences.

8. Have the groups repeat Step 7 using another statement you write on the board.

9. Pass out the reading selection for groups to read either silently or aloud.

10. Ask the groups to determine whether the text supports the two statements in Steps 7 and 8. They should be able to give evidence from the text for their decisions.

11. After Steps 1 to 10 are completed, discuss with the whole class the entire activity. The recorders should be prepared to speak for their group regarding their responses.

Inferring Main Ideas from Text

The techniques for teaching students how to infer main ideas from text that are discussed in the article "Processing Main Ideas Through Parallel Lesson Transfer," by David W. Moore and John E. Readence, are summarized and organized in the easy-to-read format on the next page. This article, from the April 1980 issue of *Journal of Reading*, explains that parallel lessons are based on the premise that once students learn how to solve a general type of problem, they can easily solve specific examples of that same type. With parallel lessons, students learn and then transfer main idea comprehension skills across related tasks of viewing pictures, listening, oral reading, and silent reading.

	Stimulus	Modeling (Teacher)	Recognition (Student)	Production (Student)
Viewing	Use interesting and rich pictures appropriate to the maturity level of learners, which can be found in magazines and newspapers.	Display several pictures, then provide and explain appropriate main idea statements about them. Note individual details so that the main ideas are apparent.	Present three or four main idea statements related to a picture with one statement containing clearly the main idea and the others being either too narrow or too broad. Have students select the best main idea statement and justify their choice.	Have students generate their own main idea statements for a picture. Then, through group discussion, ask them to select the most appropriate statement. With proficiency shown at this stage, individuals can be moved from pictures to listening.
Listening	Read aloud or play on tape a text passage. The listening selections should match students' interest, maturity, ability level, and attention span.	Model the process of generating main idea statements for the passage. Explain the main idea and how it was obtained from the listening selection.	Have students listen to passages with possible main idea statements and recognize the best choice. Justification is also important.	Ask students to generate their own main idea statements, as a group first, then individually.
Selected Oral Reading	Use interpretive reading, including choral reading of poetry, reading plays, and read-along tapes.	Model the selection of main idea after orally reading a form of interpretive reading.	Have students read selections orally and choose the main idea statements from among options given.	First have students produce their own main idea statements as a group, then individually.
Silent Reading	Use high-interest, low-vocabulary materials that are at the students' reading level.	Model the selection of main idea after silently reading easy material. As proficiency is gained move to more challenging materials.	Ask students to read selections silently and choose the main idea statements from among options given.	As a group, have students produce main idea statements. Then, have individuals do this activity on their own.

Sustained Silent Reading and Writing

In the Open to Suggestion department of the February 1990 issue of *Journal of Reading*, Valerie S. Pyle's article "SSRW—Beyond Silent Reading" discusses a technique for helping students better understand what they are reading. The Sustained Silent Reading and Writing strategy, summarized in the following adaptation, adds writing to the Sustained Silent Reading approach, a technique that promotes long periods of silent reading of self-selected material. Pyle contends that Sustained Silent Reading and Writing is the key to students' increased awareness and comprehension of the material they choose to read. This activity also helps develop students' writing abilities.

1. Have students read silently from self-selected material. They may choose reading materials according to their interests and abilities, such as novels, magazines, newspapers, and so forth.
2. After silently reading, ask students to write nonstop in a notebook for five minutes about information they have read. This causes students to stop and reflect on what they have just read.
3. Encourage students to make judgmental statements about what they are reading. Ask them to write why they enjoy a particular reading material.
4. Have students turn in their journal entries each week. Read each one of them and write brief comments.

Using Paired Storytelling to Make Sense of Text

In her article "Paired Storytelling: An Integrated Approach for EFL Students," which appeared in the Open to Suggestion section of the May 1993 issue of *Journal of Reading*, Anita Lie explains how she developed Paired Storytelling to help her English as a foreign language students use their prior knowledge to make sense of text. The Paired Storytelling approach combines reading, writing, and cooperative learning (a teaching technique described in the adaptation "Schema Theory and Cooperative Learning" in this section). Paired Storytelling not only helps students with comprehension and vocabulary development, but it also provides opportunities for one-to-one interaction among students, improves group relations, and increases self-esteem. This technique, adapted in the following steps, can be used with English as a foreign language, English as a second language, or adult literacy students.

1. Before the activity, decide how students should be paired.

2. Give a general introduction to the topic of the story chosen, write the topic on the board, then ask students what they know about the topic and how it relates to their experiences. This is intended to activate students' prior knowledge and get them ready for the story. If this brainstorming activity reveals that many stu-

dents do not have the background necessary to understand the story, then provide this information at this time.

3. Divide the story into two parts. Give the first part to one student in each pair and the second part to the other.

4. As each student reads his or her part, direct students to write the key concepts or phrases in the order in which they appear in the story.

5. Have students in each pair exchange their lists of key concepts. Give them time to relate these concepts to the story part they have read. If a student does not understand a word or phrase, ask the student who wrote that part to explain its meaning in another way or in the other student's first language.

6. Have each student develop and write his or her own account of the story by recalling the part he or she read and using the clues about the other part. Ask the reader of the first part to try to predict what will happen next and write the second part; have the reader of the second part fill in what has taken place in the first part and write it.

7. Ask students to read their stories to each other when finished.

8. Hand out the missing part of the story to the pairs and ask them to read and compare it with their versions.

9. Conclude the lesson with a discussion of the entire story either in pairs or with the whole class.

10. You may choose to give a quiz to determine how well the story was understood by all. Each student, in this case, would respond individually.

Using Text Patterns to Improve Comprehension

Claudia D. Finley and Martha N. Seaton recommend teaching students to use clues in text structure to determine the organization of content material. They maintain in their November 1987 *Journal of Reading* article "Using Text Patterns and Question Prediction to Study for Tests" that students will better comprehend reading material if they understand how the authors explain information. This adaptation outlines the authors' approach to teaching text patterns. Although Finley and Seaton used this method in their college-bound study skills class to help students prepare for a test, it can be modified and used with adult literacy students to help them read more effectively. The strategy can be taught in a two-week unit, or individual steps can be used in content-area instruction.

1. Be sure students are familiar with the following six common organizational patterns that can be found in text, outlined by Kolzow and Lehmann (1982):

    Analysis—characteristics of a concept

    Cause-effect—the results a concept produces

    Comparison-contrast—similarities and differences between concepts

    Definition—the stated meaning of a concept

    Example—specific ways a concept is used

    Sequence—the time order of events

2. As a whole class, talk about where examples of these text patterns can be found and what types of words signal the patterns. For example, words such as "first," "next," and "then" signal a certain order or sequence.

3. Provide students with unlabeled groups of words or phrases that writers use to signal a pattern as in the example in Step 2. Have them identify each group of signal words. Present paragraphs for them to search for signal words and identify the corresponding text patterns.

4. Give students topic sentences from a text and have them predict the paragraph pattern each sentence would most logically represent by noting signal words.

5. Have students identify the text's patterns of paragraphs in order to construct main idea statements. Give them a simple paragraph with the topic sentence and signal words included but content-specific words deleted (with blank lines inserted). Ask them to underline the signal words in each paragraph and then guess the main idea of the paragraph.

6. Have students use text patterns to help identify main ideas in longer text passages or a chapter. First, guide them through a chapter section, one paragraph at a time, to find main ideas. In each paragraph, have students underline signal words and the topic sentence in order to determine the paragraph's pattern.

7. Have students use patterns to predict possible test questions that might be asked about a text. With the list of section main ideas from a text chapter, they can be guided to change these ideas into questions beginning with "Who?" (definition information), "What happened?" (sequence information), "How?" (cause-effect information), and so on. Comparison-contrast and analysis patterns can be found in the way the author outlined the chapter using subheadings.

8. Encourage students to concentrate on finding the major pattern in a whole text indicated by the subheadings and their main idea questions to locate information. Once they are able to determine the pattern that the author uses to explain information, they are more likely to comprehend what they have read.

Reference
Kolzow, L.V., & Lehmann, J. (1982). *College reading: Strategies for success.* Englewood Cliffs, NJ: Prentice-Hall.

Promoting Critical Reading

It is important for students to learn how to use critical reading skills and apply them to real-life situations, so they can question what they read and understand it better. The article "Critical Reading for At-Risk Students" by Linda L. Thistlethwaite, published in the May 1990 issue of *Journal of Reading*, encourages teaching at-risk students to read critically. Thistlethwaite also reviews related research and discusses activities for teaching critical reading. These activities, which highlight questions that critical readers should ask themselves, are adapted here. See also the similar strategies "Teaching Consumer Literacy with Advertisements" and "Practicing Comprehension and Word Attack Skills with Tabloids" in Section VI.

Questioning with Tabloid Articles

1. Choose an article from a tabloid that is likely to get students' attention quickly.

2. Ask students to read the headline and predict what questions might be answered in the article.

3. Have students read the article and then write questions that they would like to ask the writer about the article.

4. Depending on the writing ability of your students, you can then direct them to write their own tabloid articles. This way students can gain further insight into the questioning nature of these articles.

Introducing Propaganda with Advertisements

1. Have students examine various magazines and newspapers to compare different types of ads and determine which basic needs are most commonly appealed to.

2. Have students design their own ads for products to understand how to use propaganda techniques such as name calling and using testimonials.

Focusing on Emotional Language in Editorials

1. Have students read an editorial and look for words that are emotional. Make editorials available that you think students will not agree with.

2. Have students rewrite each emotive sentence, deleting some of the emotional language and making each more objective. Or, you can rewrite the editorial using objective language and have

students substitute the emotional language for the objective language, making the ad directly opposite in meaning.

Using Movie Reviews to Evaluate Propaganda

1. Have students read a movie review.

2. Ask them to write the main points that the reviewer makes and determine whether each point is a fact or an opinion. Have students also search for persuasive language used by the reviewer.

3. Suggest that students then view the movie and look for the main points mentioned in the review.

4. After viewing the movie, have students write their own movie review, either individually or in pairs.

Critically Reading Newspaper Editorials

1. Select two editorials from a newspaper that present conflicting information about a subject of concern to students.

2. State the issue for students and ask them to share their first thoughts about the subject.

3. Have each student write a position statement beginning with "I believe that...." Refer to the form "Critical Reading of Editorials" beginning on the next page for recording the information requested. Variations include the following activities:

   • Direct students to read selected editorials and practice making the headlines into main idea statements.

   • Have students write individual position statements for selected issues and then read corresponding editorials to compare the writer's point of view.

- Ask students to read selected editorials and focus only on identifying examples of propaganda techniques.
- Have students read a selected set of editorials to determine the
  author's credentials, bias, and attitude toward the reader.

Critical Reading of Editorials

Initial Reaction

Issue: _____

I believe that _____

Initial Reading

Editorial #1
  What is the main idea?
  Do you agree or disagree?
  The information given
  • supports my position
  • makes me feel more strongly
    about my position
  • makes me feel less strongly
    about my position

Editorial #2
  What is the main idea?
  Do you agree or disagree?
  The information given
  • lends support to my position
  • makes me feel more strongly
    about my position
  • makes me feel less strongly
    about my position

(continued)

Critical Reading of Editorials (cont'd.)

Second Reading

Restate the main idea:	Restate the main idea:
Support statements for the main idea, and identification of each as fact or opinion:	Support statements for the main idea, and identification of each as fact or opinion:
1.	1.
2.	2.
3.	3.
Credentials of the writer:	Credentials of the writer:
Author bias:	Author bias:
Emotional language used:	Emotional language used:
Other propaganda techniques used:	Other propaganda techniques used:
Evidence of logical reasoning:	Evidence of logical reasoning:
Questions to ask the writer:	Questions to ask the writer:

Comparison—Which Editorial Was More Effective?

Which editorial impressed you most positively with its use of propaganda and other persuasive techniques?

Which was more opinion based and which was more factual?

In which were the opinions better supported with facts and examples?

Writing

Write your own editorial on this issue, keeping in mind what you liked and did not like about the editorials you evaluated. Evaluate your editorial, considering thoughts on your first and second readings.

Note: This form has been adapted from activities by Brueggeman (1986) and Cheyney (1984).

References

Brueggeman, M.A. (1986). React first, analyze second: Using editorials to teach the writing process. *Journal of Reading, 30,* 234–239.

Cheyney, A.B. (1984). *Teaching reading skills through the newspaper* (2nd ed.). Newark, DE: International Reading Association.

Improving Comprehension with Comics

Sharon Kossack and Edwina Hoffman, in their article "A Picture's Worth a Thousand Words: Comprehension Processing Via the Comics" from the Use the News department of the November 1987 issue of *Journal of Reading*, promote the use of comic strips found in newspapers to help develop students' reading comprehension abilities. The techniques listed here, which are adapted from the article, take advantage of the motivation comic strips provide because of their humor, visual context, and minimal print.

Categorizing

Have small groups of students collect comic strips and then sort them into categories (such as family, romance, animals, and so on). Allow students a chance to discuss and justify the categories assigned.

Determining the Main Idea

Distribute selected comic strips to small groups and have them reach consensus on the main ideas for the comic strips.

Comparing and Contrasting

Have students compare and contrast sets of comic strips in terms of character types, conflicts, resolutions, and traits.

Identifying Cause and Effect

Have students identify the characters involved, the problem, and the result of the problem.

Predicting Outcomes

Ask students to read all the frames in a selected comic strip except the concluding frame. Then have them predict how the strip ends and compare their version with the original concluding strip.

Teaching Summarizing Techniques to Help Comprehension

Milford A. Jeremiah's article "Summaries Improve Comprehension," from the Open to Suggestion department of the November 1988 issue of *Journal of Reading*, describes his method for teaching students to summarize text. Jeremiah contends that students can better understand what they read when they practice summarizing. Adapted in the following procedural list, this text summarization strategy, which promotes using television programs to teach summarizing techniques, works well at all instructional levels.

1. Have students, on their own, summarize a movie or televised program that they have viewed. Judge their ability to do this based on the nature of the program.

2. Suggest a list of verbs and nouns that can be used to summarize information. Examples of verbs include explain, analyze, discuss, and examine; examples of nouns are experiences, effects, processes, characteristics, and stages. Discuss the meanings of these nouns and verbs.

3. Ask students again to summarize a TV program and use the words in Step 2 in their summaries. Get consensus from the students about the TV program summaries.

4. Ask students how specific kinds of information fit into the summary.

5. When students have mastered the skill of summarizing using television programs, demonstrate to students how this same skill applies to textbooks and other reading materials.

6. Have students summarize the content of a reading assignment, applying what they have learned.

Enhancing Reading with a Modified SQ3R Technique

This is an adaptation of the modified SQ3R strategy—Survey, Question, Read, Recite, and Review—explained by Tina Jacobowitz in her article "Using Theory to Modify Practice: An Illustration with SQ3R," which appeared in the

November 1988 issue of *Journal of Reading*. The author's purpose in this article is to demonstrate how her knowledge of cognitive theory enabled her to modify and teach this study skill, and others, according to the needs of her students. She strongly emphasizes that teachers should understand the connection of theory to every study skill they teach. The SQ3R technique is designed to help readers deal effectively with new information.

Survey

1. Have students become familiar with the organization and overall contents of the reading material. After they read the title and introduction, have students ask themselves the following questions:

   How much do I already know about the topic?

   How does this topic relate to what I have studied?

   Is this topic controversial?

   What can I learn from the author about the topic?

   Are there biases about the topic?

   What do I wish to learn about the topic?

2. After reading the introduction or first paragraph, have students read the summary or the last paragraph.

3. As students read the boldface headings, ask them to list them in an outline format.

Question

1. Have students brainstorm questions related to the first part of a selection. You need to participate in this process and model good questioning.

2. Then ask students to formulate similar questions for the next part.

Read

1. Have students predict possible answers to the questions using their background knowledge and thinking abilities.

2. Direct students to read the text to confirm their predictions.

3. Have students engage in a question and answer activity similar to the television game show *Jeopardy!* For this activity, ask students to write questions in their notebooks related to the information presented in each paragraph of the textual materials.

Recite

Encourage students to enhance their understanding of the text through writing and paraphrasing the answers to the questions in the previous step.

Review

1. Have students go back to each heading and try to recall the questions and answers.

2. Have students write a summary that ties together all of the ideas they have gathered.

Comments and Notes:

SECTION IV

Developing Writing Competence

Exploring Academic Self-Perceptions Through Writing
from "Using Writing to Explore Academic Self-Perceptions"
by Hiller A. Spires

Creative Writing for Adults
from "Beyond the Barriers: Creative Writing with Adult Remedial
Students" by Sara Garfield

Promoting Writing Competence Through Letter Writing
from "Developing Writing Skills Through Letter Writing"
by Edward J. Dwyer

Writing in Journals
from "Using Student Journals in the Workplace ESL Classroom"
by Dorothy Solé

Exploring Academic Self-Perceptions Through Writing

Self-evaluation has been found to be an important element in cognitive growth. Hiller A. Spires's *Journal of Reading* article "Using Writing to Explore Academic Self-Perceptions," which appeared in the Open to Suggestion department of the April 1992 issue, suggests using a free-writing activity to help students confront perceptions they have of themselves as learners. To help students get started, Spires recommends that instructors model this process first, talking and writing about their own anxieties experienced in academic situations. This adaptation outlines the writing activity.

Direct students to write about how they view themselves as learners. They should pay particular attention to images they have of themselves in an academic setting. Ask the following questions to prompt writing:

- How do you feel about yourself as a student? Describe your strengths and weaknesses as best you can.
- How do other people (friends, co-workers, and teachers) see you as a student?
- How well have you performed in the past as a student?

63

- Have there been any major changes in your pattern of academic performance through the years? When and why did these changes occur?

- Which subjects are typically easy for you? Which ones are hard for you? Why?

- What are your interests with regard to academic settings and the learning process?

- How do you usually read and study? Where would you like to see improvement?

- What do you do when you are bored in class? Whose responsibility is it to generate interest in the class? Why?

- Who in your life has had an effect on your interest in learning? How?

- How do you feel about school and learning?

Creative Writing for Adults

This adaptation of the article "Beyond the Barriers: Creative Writing with Adult Remedial Students" by Sara Garfield details a strategy for helping students write alternative forms of poetry. Garfield's article was published in the Open to Suggestion department of the September 1993 issue of *Journal of Reading*. Her creative writing activity is useful in building students' self-esteem, provided that they understand that alternative poetry forms are not

traditional rhymed verse and that writing poetry should be fun. As with all the activities and strategies in this handbook, it should be modeled for students.

Motivating Students

Before this assignment, ask students to write a positive statement about their ability to perform the assignment such as "I, Pat, am a writer of poetry." Tell students that they will be exploring and writing different types of poems. The writing activity will be fun and easy though unlike the traditional rhymed verse. Everyone will be successful because there is no right or wrong way to write poems.

Providing Direct Instruction

Write a sample biography poem to read and display to the students on an overhead projector. Then display the formula or plan for the biography poem on the overhead projector.

Formula for Biography Poem
Line 1   first name
      2   four adjectives describing yourself in a positive way
      3   Mother (father, son, or daughter) of _____
      4   Lover of (list three items)
      5   Who feels (list three things)
      6   Who fears (list three things)
      7   Who wants to
      8   Last name

Guiding Practice

As a class, have the students create a biography poem about the whole class.

Practicing Independently

Ask students to write their own biography poems while you assist.

Sharing

Encourage students to voluntarily share their biography poems with the class.

Evaluating

Respond with positive comments about the poems, without correcting errors in spelling or mechanics. Have students indicate by writing "yes" in the upper righthand corner if they want their poems edited or shared.

Promoting Writing Competence Through Letter Writing

This strategy for promoting writing competence was adapted from Edward J. Dwyer's article "Developing Writing Skills Through Letter Writing," which appeared in the Open to Suggestion department of the December 1984 issue of *Journal of Reading*. In his article Dwyer explains how, at a residential summer school for middle school students, personal letter writing proved a good motivator for writing. He emphasizes that his students made gains in their writing skills when sustained letter writing was combined with instruction in expository writing. This strategy works well with adult literacy students.

1. Prepare students for this letter-writing activity by reviewing the format for friendly letters, including the heading, greeting, body, complimentary close, and signature. Review the correct way to address an envelope.

2. Provide a time for students to write their personal letters to friends and relatives. Treat this activity as you would sustained silent reading. Do not require students to share what they write, particularly because it is of a personal nature. If they choose to share on their own, let them do so.

3. Encourage students to proofread and correct their letters.

4. Have students send their letters.

5. Later, as students gain confidence in writing friendly letters, give them the format for a business letter, and have them begin composing letters to companies praising or complaining about specific products.

This letter-writing activity is to writing instruction as sustained silent reading is to reading instruction: both activities provide students with an opportunity to practice skills learned. See also the activity "Sustained Silent Reading and Writing" in Section III.

Writing in Journals

As Dorothy Solé explains in her article "Using Student Journals in the Workplace ESL Classroom," adult English as a second language students are often reluctant to free write on a blank journal page. This strategy, adapted from Solé's December 1990 *Journal of Reading* article in the Open to Suggestion department, provides a starting point using readings, class discussions, and other personal experiences to support students in their journal writing.

1. Arrange your class or tutoring session around a general theme or unit for continuity of instruction.

2. Select an interesting reading with which students can identify.

3. Following the reading, allow time for students to react and exchange or share ideas about the topic.

4. On the chalkboard, write a series of specific "wh" questions related to the theme of the class and directed personally to the students. For example, if the theme is travel, then include such questions as "Where did you go?" "What mode of transportation did you use?" "What did you enjoy the most?" "What aggravated you the most?" "Why were you aggravated?" "Who went with you?" and "What will you remember from this trip, more than anything else?"

5. Inform students that all the questions do not have to be answered nor must they be answered in any order. These questions serve as a springboard to activate their minds to think.

6. Finally, direct students to begin writing in their journals, keeping in mind their thoughts about and reactions to the reading and the "wh" questions.

Précis Writing

Research suggests that the development of writing skills can enhance the development of reading skills. In the article "Précis Writing: Promoting Vocabulary Development and Comprehension," from the March 1983 *Journal of Reading* issue, Karen D'Angelo outlines the specific tasks involved in précis writing—a summary of the main points of an original work, usually less than one-third the length of the original. She discusses how these tasks promote reading comprehension and vocabulary development, and she presents ways of teaching these tasks. The following steps in précis writing are adapted from the article.

It is important to note that the précis—or summary—of a text results from the following activities that include selecting topic sentences, identifying the location of topic sentences within paragraphs, using synonyms, and rephrasing. To write an accurate and brief précis, encourage students to remember to identify topic sentences, rephrase sentences in their own words, and keep the correct sequence of the text as they write.

Identifying Main Ideas

1. Reproduce paragraphs or short selections from content area or nonfiction materials and have students identify orally and then underline sentences containing main or important ideas. Work along with the students, leading them to look for the most general sentence in the paragraph. The remaining sentences will include specific supporting information. You may need to model examples of general ideas and specific ideas to help students grasp the concept.

2. After identifying the main ideas in the paragraphs, have students note the possible location of topic sentences in paragraphs using the following graphic shapes developed by Burmeister (1974):

$\triangledown$ topic sentence at beginning of paragraph

$\triangle$ topic sentence at end of paragraph

$\rhd\!\!\lhd$ topic sentences at beginning and end

$\diamondsuit$ topic sentence within paragraph

$\bigcirc$ topic sentence not stated

Paraphrasing and Writing Ideas

1. Have students in small groups think of synonyms for key words in topic sentences. (Here is an excellent opportunity to incorporate dictionary and thesaurus use.)

2. Ask students to paraphrase the topic sentences orally and to discuss choices.

3. Have students write their paraphrased ideas after input has been received from the group.

Reference
Burmeister, L.E. (1974). *Reading strategies for secondary school teachers*. Reading,
MA: Addison-Wesley.

Précis Writing and Critical Reading

This adaptation of Dwight Porter's February 1990 article "Précis Writing in the ESL Classroom," from the Open to Suggestion department of *Journal of Reading*, stresses the potential that précis writing has for English as a second language students. In the ESL classroom and the regular classroom this type of writing, explained in the previous strategy, develops abstracting and synthesizing skills and can improve critical reading. The following adaptation of Porter's article is another procedure for using précis writing with adult literacy students.

1. Have students read and summarize a short narrative passage.
2. Ask students to exchange and read each other's summaries.
3. Present a model précis of the passage on an overhead projector, and ask students to compare and contrast their summaries with the model.
4. Discuss précis writing and its usefulness, based on the information given in the previous strategy, "Précis Writing."

5. Present a second narrative passage. Have students compose a précis in groups and evaluate each group's work.

6. After students have written an acceptable group précis, have them compose an individual précis writing from a short passage.

7. Have students then move from short passages to longer selections based on their skill development.

8. When students have demonstrated success with using narrative passages, have them work with expository or content area text.

Short Stories and Writing

The following step-by-step strategy, adapted from the March 1992 *Journal of Reading* article "Continuing Fun with Short Stories and Writing," can be used to motivate students' engagement with a short story and enhance their understanding and enjoyment of writing. The article, which appeared in the Open to Suggestion department, was written by Constance Lessaris Fellios.

1. Choose a published short story or an excerpt and give only the first paragraph to one student. Ask the student to write a second paragraph to add to the first one.

2. Remove the first paragraph, present the second paragraph to another student, and ask him or her to add a subsequent paragraph.

3. Continue this process until all students have written one paragraph and have completed the story. Allow each student 15 to 20 minutes to write a paragraph so that attention can be focused on organization and conciseness. The other students should proceed with other activities while one student at a time writes in another location or in an undisturbed area of the room.

4. When all students are finished writing, photocopy and distribute the complete story. Have students discuss their writing and how each addition affects the whole story.

5. Read aloud the original published short story to the students. Lead a discussion of its theme and purpose.

6. Assign a follow-up writing activity that relates to the original short story such as an analysis of a character or author's viewpoint.

These steps could be varied in the following way:

1. Divide students into three or four groups and let each group work with a different short story. As before, give one student in the group the first paragraph of the story.

2. Have individuals of each group add a single paragraph to the one before.

3. Ask the groups to share their stories with the class, and then, as a whole class, discuss the original short stories. In this variation, students will complete their written stories faster, and more pieces of literature can be covered.

Strategies for Correcting Writing Errors

Several strategies for making corrections to adult students' writing are summarized in this adaptation of Pat Best's article "Correcting Adult Students' Writing Errors," which appeared in the Open to Suggestion department of the November 1990 issue of *Journal of Reading*. These techniques for correcting errors are nonthreatening and constructive.

- Acknowledge adult students' wealth of knowledge and life experience that they bring to the writing process. Both provide an interesting forum for sharing ideas.

- Make no writing corrections at first. Build confidence by asking students to write about familiar topics related to home, family, and work. Focus on the content and communication only. Respond conversationally in writing.

- Mark only one type of error per assignment after students have completed several writing assignments, thus keeping the correction tasks manageable.

- Allow the students to make their own corrections as much as possible. Write prompting questions on students' assignments that will guide students in making the proper corrections. Draw a line under the sentence parts that need correcting. For example, if spelling is the error being emphasized for an assignment, simply draw a line under the misspelled word for students to correct.

Using Computers in Adult Literacy Writing Programs

The article "Integrating Computers into Adult Literacy Programs" by Deborah Young and Martha Irwin, published in the April 1988 issue of *Journal of Reading,* describes ways in which word processors and databases can be used in a literacy program. Young and Irwin emphasize that this technology should be integrated in ways that are consistent with an interactive theory of reading—that is, meaning should be constructed from the students' existing knowledge, the information suggested by the written language, and the context of the written situation. Use of computers in literacy programs should also take into consideration the backgrounds and interests of the students. The following strategies, which can be used in an adult writing program, are adapted from the article.

Writing an Original Text

1. Have a small group of students generate ideas about a topic. The brainstorming of ideas might be based on reactions to something that has been read to them or by them.
2. Have students record ideas on the word processor.
3. Print out copies for each student in the group, so they can think about the ideas during the prewriting stage.

4. Have students write an original text, such as a friendly letter or an experience story, based on the ideas generated. This can be done on paper first, or it can be entered directly into the computer. The main issue is for students to express their ideas.

5. Allow students to write thoughts without regard for spelling or grammar. These can be corrected later on the word processor.

6. As students write, offer special instruction for editorial needs such as dealing with grammar or punctuation.

7. Once the students' writings are retained on disk, create the following related lessons from them:

Vocabulary expansion. Have students use the search and replace feature of the word processing program to substitute synonyms for certain words.

Context clue usage. Direct students to use the word processing program to delete key words in passages and insert blanks to be completed by other students.

Idea alternative. Have students create new endings for open-ended sentences presented.

Recording Predictions about Texts

1. Choose a story with a topic that interests students.

2. Link reading, writing, and computers by using the word processor to store students' predictions, background knowledge, and questions about the topic.

3. After students read the text, have them make comparisons between the initial information stored and the actual text.

Ideas for Using Finished Writings

- Compile finished products in a notebook.
- Use finished writings as free reading material.
- Feature selected writings in a newspaper or newsletter format for wider distribution.
- Have students share their writing with others.

Comments and Notes:

SECTION V

Increasing
Vocabulary

An Independent Word-Learning Strategy

In her article "The Vocabulary Self-Collection Strategy: An Active Approach to Word Learning," Martha Rapp Haggard contends that teaching efforts to promote vocabulary development should satisfy two conditions: instruction should be directed toward those words students need to know, and it should give students the skills necessary for independent vocabulary growth. Haggard's article from the December 1982 issue of *Journal of Reading* meets these conditions with its emphasis on context. An adaptation of the Vocabulary Self-Collection Strategy is outlined here.

1. Ask students to bring to class one word (general or content related) that they think the class should learn.
2. Have students write their word on the chalkboard and tell what it means; students should also tell where each word was found and why they think the word should be learned.
3. Ask other students to add any information they can to each meaning.
4. Direct students to consult references for word meanings that are incomplete. Confirm final meanings.
5. Have students eliminate duplicate words on the list and words that they already know.
6. Have students record the class word list along with agreed-upon meanings.

81

7. Allow students to include any additional words they have found in context on their personal vocabulary lists.

8. Assign follow-up study activities for use with the class list such as using the words in sentences or paragraphs and finding synonyms or antonyms.

9. Evaluate students' progress in learning the new words at the end of the week. Evaluation may include the spelling, definition, and use of the words.

Using External Context Clues to Learn Vocabulary

It has been found that students' use of context may be responsible for most of their vocabulary learning at all grade levels. Randall James Ryder, in his article "Teaching Vocabulary Through External Context Clues" from the October 1986 issue of *Journal of Reading*, describes an instructional approach for teaching external clues—syntactic and semantic elements within and among sentences. This approach is based on three assumptions: (1) students learn best when teachers proceed from concrete to abstract vocabulary; (2) context clues should be taught with classroom text; and (3) student mastery varies with text difficulty. The three stages of this teaching technique are outlined in this adaptation.

Stage One—Visual Context Clues

1. Display a sentence containing a word (a verb is the easiest to begin with) that is unknown by most students. Read the sentence aloud and underline the new word.

2. Show a picture containing people that provides a clue to the word's meaning.

3. Direct students to examine the picture in light of the sentence and to list actions being taken by people in the picture.

4. Write the list of words where they can be seen by all students. Point out the pictorial clues in the picture, which will lead to the unknown word.

5. Direct students to give their individual meaning of the unknown word.

6. Ask students to identify those pictorial clues that helped them determine the meaning of the unknown word.

7. Exhibit fewer and fewer visual clues as students grasp this activity. Lead students to find clues within the sentence.

8. Have students move to stage two when they have reached an acceptable level of performance with this task.

Stage Two—Sentence Context

1. Present sentences containing a chosen word's meaning. Read the sentences aloud, identify the unknown word, and define it. Have students look for clues in the sentence that aid in obtaining meanings for the word.

2. Present new vocabulary in sentences that show fewer direct context clues. Again, read the sentence, provide the meaning, and then ask students to locate the clues.

3. Give multiple sentences, each with a clue to a word's meaning. The unknown word should appear in only one of the sentences. Have students locate the clues.

Stage Three—Paragraph Context

1. Underline key context clues in a paragraph from a written text. Ask students to define the unknown word on the basis of the underlined context clues. Reverse this procedure by first defining the unknown word then asking students to locate and identify those clues in the paragraph that give meaning to the unknown word.

2. Direct students to focus on key words and phrases within several paragraphs that will aid in the meaning of a word. Underline these context clues, then ask students to define the word from the clues.

Creating and Using Word Banks

A "word bank" is a list of words that have been accumulated to build sight vocabulary. This adaptation of Lynne Austin-Anglea's article "Word Banks for Adult Literacy," from the Open to Suggestion department of the December 1990 issue of *Journal of Reading*, offers strategies for developing word banks and using them to build vocabulary, practice spelling, and develop critical thinking skills. These strategies can be used with one student or a class.

1. Have students select a topic of interest such as cooking.

2. Say to them, "When I think of cooking I think of foods. What do you think of?" Continue this question and response activity, following up on the responses, until the word bank includes 30 to 50 words (depending on knowledge of topic).

3. Record both your responses and the students' responses.

4. Use the supply of words (word bank) in a variety of language activities to make the words into a working vocabulary for the students. Suggested activities include the following:

   • Look for clusters of words or words that fit into certain categories, for example, vegetable dishes, meat dishes, or types of cooking. Create a semantic or word map of these categories with accompanying words. (See the example on the following page.)

   • Add prefixes and suffixes to selected words in the word bank. Build on the word "boil" (type of cooking) to create words such as parboil, boiling, boiled, boils. Discuss how changing the form can change the meaning or use of the word.

   • Use the word bank as a prereading or prewriting activity. Have students dictate or write a story using selected words from the word bank. Review words and meaning before reading or writing the story.

   • Write words on small cards or notebook paper for easy accessibility and storage. Add new words to the word bank as they are introduced through reading and conversation.

   • Plan a writing activity using words from the word bank. Determine a pattern of organization according to the purpose of the writing, for example, descriptive, sequential, cause and effect, and so on. (See also the strategy "Using Text Patterns to

Improve Comprehension" in Section III for more information on text organization.)

• Focus on spelling by noting the word parts (prefixes, suffixes, endings, and roots) as aids to spelling correctly. Demonstrate how division of word parts simplifies spelling; for instance, break the word "comprehension" into syllables to read com/pre/hen/sion.

Word Map for "Cooking" Topic

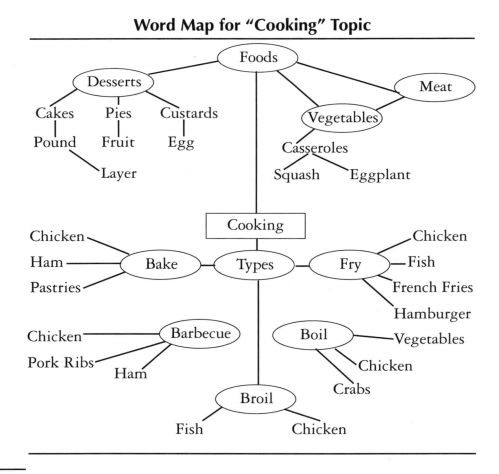

Vowel-Sound-Stick Method of Syllabication

This strategy for pronouncing unfamiliar words is adapted from the article "Vowel-Sound-Stick: Word Attack for Secondary Remedial Students" by Gayla Sellers, published in the October 1988 issue of *Journal of Reading*. Adult literacy students may become frustrated when reading if they cannot pronounce words that are not in their vocabulary. Sellers explains a technique that students can use to enable them to read almost any word they come across without a dictionary or other help. This method allows for some phonics instruction to help pronunciation and word identification. The "stick" in this method refers to the vertical line or slash drawn between syllables in words.

Steps in the Vowel-Sound-Stick Strategy

1. Have students begin at the right of the word and move left.
2. Direct students to look for the vowel, then the "sound" (the consonant or consonant cluster), then place the stick.
3. Indicate that students should place a v over each vowel and an s over each sound—for example, /stu/dent

Rules to Remember When Using the Vowel-Sound-Stick Method

- Prefixes and suffixes are separate syllables and should be noted with a stick (slash mark) first—for example, *un/able*.

- Consonant blends or clusters are never separated but stay together in one syllable—for instance, *(bl)end*.

- Compound words are always divided—*over/head*.

- Double consonants are divided in the middle—*ap/pear*.

- The *-ed* ending is a different syllable only when it comes after a *d* or a *t*—*divid/ed*.

- Vowels are *a*, *e*, *i*, *o*, and *u*. When *y* ends a word or appears in the middle of a word it is a vowel—*reply*, *hydrogen*.

- When double vowels exist, circle them and try them together first. Try a stick between the double vowels if the word is not known—*really*, *re/ality*

- When a word ends in *e*, assume that it is a silent *e* with no sound—*se/clude*.

- Endings with *-le* such as */ble*, */gle*, and */dle* are considered syllables of their own—*ta/ble*.

A Vocabulary Game

Joan Ruddiman has developed a vocabulary game that not only gives her middle school students strategies to figure out the meaning of words in isolation but also empowers them to take charge of their own learning. Following is a summary of Ruddiman's vocabulary game, which is adapted from her article "The Vocab Game: Empowering Students Through Word Awareness" from the Open to Suggestion department of the February 1993 issue of *Journal of Reading*. This strategy can be used with students of any age.

Guidelines and Points System

- If a student or group fails to produce a word, the class or group loses five points.
- The word is presented to the teacher in isolation without any context clues. If the teacher fails to identify the word, the class gets five points. If any other students know the meaning, the class gets five points.
- The class gets a reward when they reach 100 points.

The Vocab Game Procedures

1. Have each student present a word for the week on the designated "Vocab Day." If class is large (10 or more), small groups of 4 to 6 students may work together. The words should be from magazines, novels, newspapers, or other material, and students should give the source of the words and how the words are used in context.

2. Direct students to examine each word for meaning, etymology, and part of speech through use of the dictionary. (Dictionaries will need to be available for each group for this activity.)

3. Have each group choose one word to present to you. The objective here is for students to "stump" the teacher.

4. Appoint a scorekeeper to keep a running score sheet (posted on

the bulletin board) for the class. A recorder is also needed to write what is said on the chalkboard during the games.

5. Have the recorder spell out on the board each word that is presented by each student or group.

6. Indicate whether or not you know the word.

7. Direct students from the other groups to give possible meanings of the word.

8. Try to define the word by modeling an analysis: separate affixes, identify roots, and explain possible usage of the word. Then arrive at the meaning of the word.

9. Have individual students or the group read the dictionary meaning. Points are given as necessary and recorded by the scorekeeper.

10. Examine the etymology of the word and relate it to the meaning.

11. Discuss history, historical meanings, related interests, and related words, depending on the given word.

12. Discuss how the word was used in context and where it was found.

13. Find synonyms and antonyms for the word and use analogies when possible.

14. Periodically provide students with a complete word list containing all the information on each word (from recorder's notes) for study and review.

Using Structured Overviews to Teach Content Area Terms

In their article "Structured Overviews for Teaching Science Concepts and Terms," which appeared in the Open to

Suggestion department of the *Journal of Reading* December 1992 issue, Ronald Wolfe and Alice Lopez discuss a middle school project that resulted from their combined efforts as a reading teacher and a science teacher. To help students learn science terminology and concepts, these teachers used structured overviews of the vocabulary in a reading assignment. This adaptation of the article describes five of the methods Wolfe and Lopez used to present overviews to their students. These methods would also work well with adult literacy students and can be used to teach terminology in other curriculum areas.

Using the Overhead Projector

1. Plan a vocabulary or concept overview prior to the lesson.
2. Using an overhead projector and transparency, show the students, item by item, how the overview was developed. Write the words on the transparency and ask students how these words might be related. With student involvement, the overview is constructed on the transparency.
3. Have students copy the structured overview into their notebooks to use as a model.

Preparing Sentence Strips

Construct a bulletin board display using target words written on sentence strips. The space can determine the amount of detail to be included: small bulletin boards may include just a basic overview;

larger boards could contain the basic overview, and you could have students supply the details.

Working with Note Cards and Small Groups

1. Divide students into small groups and give each group note cards with key words for the current reading assignment.

2. Allow each group, with a leader, to plan cooperatively its own overview.

3. When all groups complete their tasks, ask group leaders to share their overviews with the rest of the class. Transparency sheets may be given to each group for use in sharing.

Designating a Group

1. Assign a small group of students to develop a structured overview for the rest of the class.

2. Have the group read the assignment, agree on an overview structure, and draw it on rolled chart paper.

3. Direct the group to select a reporter to share the completed overview with the class.

Doing Their Own

After students have had adequate experience with structured overviews, ask them to read a selection and create their own versions on notebook paper. These papers can then be circulated among the class for sharing, or you can let students share in pairs.

Vocabulary Development
Through Newspaper Articles

This strategy for vocabulary development is adapted from the article "Vocabulary Teaching: An Investment in Literacy," which appeared in the April 1986 issue of *Journal of Reading*. In this article authors Donna G. Laffey and James L. Laffey describe a vocabulary lesson that was part of a project designed to teach economic concepts through the newspaper to remedial middle school readers. The authors note that they believe that the sequence in which vocabulary lessons are organized and taught depends on teachers' knowledge of their students and the subject matter. The newspaper articles used in this lesson should be of interest to the students being taught.

1. Preselect words to be taught from relevant newspaper articles before giving the articles to students.
2. List the words either on the chalkboard, a transparency, or a handout.
3. Pronounce each of the words first, then have students pronounce each word. Follow this exercise by defining each word.
4. Have students read the article softly aloud to themselves, and then discuss the words in the context of the article. Have them relate the new vocabulary words to their background of experiences and share these experiences with the class.

93

5. Present the words to the students a second time, in a "structured overview" format—meaningfully organized on a chalkboard, transparency, or handout.

6. Review the words in a discussion emphasizing the relationships among the terms.

7. Have students complete a matching exercise, matching words to their definition, as a review and reinforcement activity.

8. Provide students with a guide that explains the use of the new vocabulary in context, with which they can interact with the text and other students.

Vocabulary Development Through Cartoons and Comics

Bobbye S. Goldstein's April 1986 *Journal of Reading* article "Looking at Cartoons and Comics in a New Way" discusses ways in which vocabulary can be taught with cartoons and comics from the newspaper to students of any language or ethnic group. Goldstein also notes that these ideas are suitable for both monolingual and bilingual students. The following strategies for helping students develop vocabulary, which have been adapted from the article, should draw an enthusiastic response from adult literacy students.

1. Discuss with students the distinctive features of cartoons and comics, including the following:

   typeface

   number of frames

   type of comic or cartoon (political or humorous)

   location of comic (editorial or comics page)

   type of visual clues (for example, a light bulb indicates an idea)

   use of balloons to show someone is speaking

   main characters' consistency of appearance

   use of humor

   human characteristics of animals

2. Have students keep notebooks, journals, or vocabulary cards on a regular basis for the vocabulary found in comics. Words can be divided into categories such as figurative language and colloquial expressions (of great benefit to ESL students). Discuss the meaning of the words or expressions in the humorous context, and then have students write the expressions along with meanings into their notebook or on vocabulary cards.

3. Have students locate and record puns (for example, "What is black and white and *read* all over?—a newspaper"), palindromes (words or sentences that read the same backward and forward, as "lion oil"), and multiple meanings of words.

4. Allow students to share information found with the class once or twice a week. The search for vocabulary words or expressions in comics and cartoons is an ongoing process. A bulletin board display may also be another way to share interesting words found.

5. Have students who are interested develop their own cartoons and comics.

Comments and Notes:

SECTION VI

Using Alternative
Reading Materials

Using Picture Books in Adult Literacy Programs
from "Picture Books in the Adult Literacy Curriculum" by Peggy A. Sharp

The Shared Book Experience
from "Bigger Is Better: Shared Book Experience with Adults"
by Karen Hicks & Beth Wadlington

Using Magazines for Teaching
from "Magazines in the Classroom: Beyond Recreational Reading"
by Mary W. Olson, Thomas C. Gee, & Nora Forester

Reading Classic Novels with Adult New Readers
from "Using Classic Novels with Adult New Readers"
by Jane McCabe Schierloh

Teaching Consumer Literacy with Advertisements
from "Consumer Advocacy, Empowerment, and Adult Literacy"
by La Vergne Rosow

Practicing Comprehension and Word Attack Skills with Tabloids
from "Using the *National Enquirer* with Unmotivated or Language-
Handicapped Readers" by Carol LaSasso

Using Annual Reports in the Workplace
from "Using Annual Reports for Adult Literacy Improvement"
by Phyllis A. Miller

Using Picture Books in Adult Literacy Programs

In her article "Picture Books in the Adult Literacy Curriculum," which appeared in the *Journal of Reading* November 1991 issue, Peggy A. Sharp argues that "an adult literacy program based on reading children's picture books can emphasize learners' roles as competent parents, rather than their roles as deficient readers." Sharp also notes that in addition to helping adults learn to read, a literacy program should also teach techniques that learners can use when sharing picture books with their children. The article gives specific suggestions for teaching these techniques and lists some recommended books to use with students. The following adaptation of Sharp's article offers a strategy for using picture books with adults.

1. Have adult students think of story books they remember from their childhood. If possible, locate these stories and read them aloud to the group.

2. After students have discussed their memories of favorite stories and heard the stories reread, introduce new stories for students to practice reading aloud. Paired reading (Johnson & Louis, 1990) can be used for this practice activity with each partner serving both as reader and listener and supporting the other.

3. When students feel comfortable with reading the book aloud to children, have them plan ways to draw children into the story. For

example, if a word or line is repeated throughout the story, have them encourage children to participate. If the story is about popcorn, then popcorn could be provided as children discuss the story.

Reference

Johnson, T.D., & Louis, D.R. (1990). *Bringing it all together: A program for literacy*. Portsmouth, NH: Heinemann.

The Shared Book Experience

The following teaching technique serves to provide adults with high-quality literature to read and enjoy and, at the same time, develop their language skills naturally. The technique is adapted from an article in the Open to Suggestion department of the February 1994 issue of *Journal of Reading*. The article "Bigger Is Better: Shared Book Experience with Adults," written by Karen Hicks and Beth Wadlington, highlights the Shared Book Experience, which is an interesting way to help foster good reading habits. To use this strategy, Hicks and Wadlington point out that choosing the right book is crucial: it must be interesting and relevant to students' lives, and it should contain descriptive and figurative language.

1. Choose an interesting book for this strategy. Introduce students to the parts of the book, the author, and the illustrator, and give

a brief overview of the story. From the overview, give students a purpose for listening: for example, say, "Listen to find out what happens to _____."

2. Read aloud 15 to 20 minutes while students read along from pages that have been made into transparencies and projected on an overhead projector. (This makes the Big Book appearance.)

3. Guide the reading of each line with a pointer gliding underneath the words so that everyone can keep up with the place.

4. As you read the words aloud, have students repeat words or phrases that are known. Familiarize yourself with the story before reading it aloud so that you demonstrate proper expression and observance of punctuation cues.

5. Make periodic stops throughout the story to ask questions, reread passages, and discuss word meanings to emphasize that reading is meant to be meaningful. The students (or listeners) have a chance to learn new vocabulary, punctuation cues, letter-sound relationships, good sentence structure, and directionality.

6. Allow students time to predict meanings of words within the story. Check predictions by rereading the passage and inserting synonyms or definitions given or by using the dictionary as a last resort.

7. After reading, begin the discussion with the stated purpose given in Step 1. Follow with other questions about the story content to determine how well students understood the story and whether they liked the story.

8. As a follow-up activity, demonstrate writing the book's plot on the left side of a piece of paper with individual comments on the right side. Have students write their personal reactions to the story, and tell them you will read the comments for meaning only.

101

Using Magazines for Teaching

Using magazines as a supplemental instructional material in the classroom helps students with reading skill development and provides a motivation to read because magazines include high-interest articles, attractive text layout, and descriptive language. This list of activities for using magazines with students is adapted from the article "Magazines in the Classroom: Beyond Recreational Reading" by Mary W. Olson, Thomas C. Gee, and Nora Forester. The article appeared in the May 1989 issue of *Journal of Reading* and also provides a comprehensive list of magazines that are appropriate for classroom use and can be used in tutoring sessions.

- Encourage students to evaluate what they read in terms of authors' credentials, timeliness of information, thoroughness of treatment, purposes for writing, and sources of information.

- Help students summarize the main points of an article by having them create a semantic web or graphic overview of the article's content. Summaries can then be written from the web or overview.

- Encourage students to write editors or writers in response to an article they liked or disliked. Through such a response, they learn to be critical readers.

- Ask students to analyze a writer's craft by examining the organization of an article, the paragraph development, the author's language, the author's use of examples and illustrations, the purpose of the opening and closing paragraphs, and other elements of composition. Good writing skills can be modeled from well-chosen articles.

- Help students develop a strategy for reading that includes activating prior knowledge, predicting what an article is about, and relating the content to their own experiences.

- Ask students to brainstorm, before reading an article, what they already know about the topic. Have them predict what will be discussed. While reading, ask them to determine if their predictions were correct and note new information found. After reading, students can weigh their predictions, summarize the article, and determine the relevancy of the new information.

- Have students use the paired storytelling strategy described in Section III with selected magazine articles.

Reading Classic Novels with Adult New Readers

Because adult literacy learners often have much broader goals for learning how to read than day-to-day survival or job readiness, Jane McCabe Schierloh advocates offering whole selections of well-written literature to students for their enjoyment in her article "Using Classic Novels with Adult New Readers," from the May 1992 *Journal of Reading* issue. Schierloh describes how, in an adult basic education class in which she has been involved, teachers have used adapted or abridged classic novels by first reading aloud short passages to students. By reading silently along with the teacher, students see good reading modeled and can enjoy novels. This strategy, along with guidelines for selecting adapted novels and excerpts, is outlined in the following adaptation of the *Journal of Reading* article.

Simple Lesson Plan Steps to Use with Each Novel

1. Begin each class with a brief review of the plot to date to help tie the story together.
2. Provide copies of the excerpt for students to follow along silently as you read aloud.
3. Hold a discussion of the part of the novel read.
4. Study vocabulary—pronunciation and meaning—from the novel.
5. Have students read the excerpt orally, then engage them in another discussion.
6. Read aloud an excerpt from the original novel.
7. Discuss a writing question derived from the novel.
8. Have students engage in a writing activity.

Guidelines for Selecting Adapted Novels

- Students' background knowledge must be considered.
- Sentence structure must flow naturally and be easy to comprehend.
- Complex plots should allow the reader to move slowly.
- Characters should be developed enough to interest the reader.
- New characters should be introduced slowly so that the reader can remember them from one page to the next.

Guidelines for Selecting Excerpts

- Dialogue (narrative) passages should be chosen rather than descriptive passages because the vocabulary, sentences, and emotional intensity are easier for students to understand.

- Scenes should involve exciting action to be effective.

- Characterization should be strong enough to hold the attention of students.

- Excerpts should be brief and easy to read without much explanation.

Teaching Consumer Literacy with Advertisements

All students should be taught consumer education—how to analyze the information that influences everyday life. In her article "Consumer Advocacy, Empowerment, and Adult Literacy," La Vergne Rosow discusses how she used advertisements and junk mail promotions with her multicultural, multilingual, and multiaged students to promote critical thinking. She also explains how teaching consumer advocacy fits well with current thought on learning theory. The following teaching strategy, which also serves to empower students, is adapted from Rosow's article from the December 1990 issue of *Journal of Reading*.

1. Encourage students to collect newspaper ads and junk mail promotions to use as reading material in the classroom.

2. Review with students the seven most common propaganda techniques of name calling, glittering generalities, plain folks, transfer, testimonial, bandwagon, and card stacking.

3. When students have become familiar with the propaganda techniques, have them sort their collected ads and promotions according to the techniques.

4. Have students examine the sorted material critically and express their opinions about them orally (with partner) and in written language.

5. Have students write promotional materials for a product or service that they might try to sell in the future. Students may use reference materials such as ads, a dictionary, a thesaurus, or other sources to develop honest and productive ads.

Practicing Comprehension and Word Attack Skills with Tabloids

As mentioned in previous strategies, the newspaper is an excellent source of printed material for adult literacy students. Tabloids such as the *National Enquirer* are similar to newspapers because they are inexpensive, readily available, and have an easy-to-read format, yet because of their attention-getting headlines they can sometimes better entice reluctant readers to interact with print. In a March 1983

Journal of Reading article entitled "Using the *National Enquirer* with Unmotivated or Language-Handicapped Readers," author Carol LaSasso argues that, although not ideal for all students, tabloids can be used successfully with some students. This adaptation of LaSasso's article lists the skills that can be practiced through the use of a tabloid.

Practicing Reading Comprehension Skills

Have students do the following exercises:

- locate certain information to support main idea or confirm predictions
- judge fact from opinion in an article
- draw conclusions from reading headlines
- interpret pictures or headlines
- analyze the credibility of an author's informational sources
- skim and scan based on reading purposes

Using Word Attack Skills

Have students practice the following to determine word meanings:

- identify compound words
- identify prefixes and suffixes
- interpret abbreviations and punctuation
- use context clues
- expand word meaning
- identify figurative language

Other Ways to Use Tabloids

- Buy multiple copies of a tabloid each week, and select, clip, mount, and file interesting articles to use in practicing the skills mentioned.
- File tabloid articles according to specific skill development.
- Keep a few whole copies of tabloids for use for free reading.

Using Annual Reports in the Workplace

Although many adult students have mastered basic reading skills, they still need assistance in transferring this knowledge to complex reading materials that require a great deal of inferential thinking and problem solving. Materials such as the annual reports found in the workplace often look appealing and interesting, but they are seldom read because of the complexity of contents. In the article "Using Annual Reports for Adult Literacy Improvement," which appears in the October 1988 issue of *Journal of Reading*, Phyllis A. Miller describes the use and format of annual business reports and gives suggestions for using them with students. The following adaptation of her strategy lists planning and implementation steps for instructing students with annual reports.

Planning Stage

1. Review several annual reports with attention to general content and structure. Start with the public library as a source.

2. Compare annual reports from a similar industry.

3. Select a report and apply the following implementation stage steps to become familiar with the procedure.

4. Choose the reports to be used with students. Request multiple copies from companies, and be sure to indicate that they will be used for educational purposes.

5. Compile an assortment of annual reports to use with students.

6. Develop lesson plans centered around the reports. If working with a particular company, use that company's report first, then move to competitors' reports.

Implementation Stage

1. Have students read to find out the general content and structure of the report.

2. Discuss and set purposes for reading the report. Have students think of questions to be answered from the report.

3. Ask students to obtain meaning of unfamiliar financial terms.

4. Direct students to skim the footnotes and the summary at end of report for key information and explanations.

5. Have students read the beginning of the report, which often is the chairman's letter, to discover the status of the company and future projections. Have them continue to search through other pages for new or different directions given by company personnel.

6. Help students examine the section on numbers, beginning with the balance sheet. Compare the current assets with current lia-

bilities to obtain the net working capital. Have students do the following optional activities with this section:

- Compare an annual report of one year with the previous year.

- Look at the balance sheet and compare the stockholders' equity (the difference between all assets and liabilities) from one year to the next.

- Compare the longterm debt to that of an earlier year or to other similar companies.

- Compare the sales at the top of the income statement with sales of the previous year.

- Notice the expenses and the net income. Pay attention to footnotes that may provide an explanation for increases or decreases.

Comments and Notes:

Conclusion

It has been a great and rewarding challenge for me to review, adapt, and use selected strategies found in the *Journal of Reading* that are pertinent to adult literacy. Although this book includes many strategies that adult literacy tutors will find extremely helpful, IRA's *Journal of Reading*—now called *Journal of Adolescent & Adult Literacy*—contains many more innovative and appropriate articles that detail teaching strategies to be used with adult literacy learners.

I shall conclude by offering an original poem that partly summarizes what this handbook is about.

Tips at Your Fingertips

"Tips at your fingertips"
Is just another way to say,
You don't have to read every journal
To find an innovative way
To read, write, listen, or speak
And use cooperative learning, too.
It is all here before you,
Just choose which you want to do.

Strategies can be adapted
To all levels of learning, you see.
So get to know your adult learners,
Before you choose the strategy.

This can be done in many ways;
Take the time and experiment.
It's worth your time and effort,
Go ahead and let them invent
The spelling of various words
Will be easy for them to read
Because they already know the meaning,
Just let them take the lead.

There are alternative reading materials
For you to pick and choose,
But be sure the purposes are known
Before you begin to use.
So, when you need a new strategy
And your lesson planning dips,
Just reach to your bookshelf
And pull *Tips at Your Fingertips*!

APPENDIX A   Adult Basic Word List

The following Adult Basic Word List from the December 1984 *Journal of Reading* article "First Steps Toward an Adult Basic Word List," by Elaine G. Wangberg, Bruce Thompson, and Justin E. Levitov, is presented as a spelling and writing reference for adult learners reading between the first and fifth grade level. The authors generated this list from computer analysis of the words most frequently written by 22 illiterate adults who participated in a series of interactive language experience approach microcomputer lessons. Words with an asterisk (*) were used 50 or more times. Words in boldface type occurred 10 or more times. All other words appeared 5 to 9 times. This list can also be used by teachers and tutors for adult literacy lessons and curriculum design.

*a	always	ask	*be
*about	*am	at	beach
after	an	away	beat
again	*and	baby	beautiful
airplane	any	**back**	*because
*all	anything	bad	bed
alone	*are	ball	**been**
along	around	baseball	**before**
also	as	basketball	being

best	**cooks**	favor	grade
better	**could**	**favorite**	great
Bible	country	**feel**	**had**
big	**daddy**	feeling	happiness
bike	dancing	few	**happy**
blue	*day	fire	**hard**
boy	days	**first**	**has**
boyfriend	dead	fishing	**have**
bring	did	flowers	having
brothers	**didn't**	flying	*he
bus	dinner	food	head
*but	*do	football	**heart**
buy	does	*for	**help**
by	doesn't	forget	her
call	**dog**	**friend**	here
came	**doing**	**friends**	**high**
*can	*don't	from	**him**
can't	**down**	fun	his
car	**dream**	gave	hobbies
care	**dreams**	G.E.D.	hobby
chance	drive	*get	holiday
child	**each**	getting	**holidays**
children	easy	girl	home
Christmas	**eat**	girls	*hope
church	end	**give**	hopes
city	**enjoy**	*go	**house**
close	enjoyed	God	houses
color	**every**	*going	**how**
come	everything	*good	hurt
coming	**family**	goodbye	**husband**
cook	fast	**got**	*I

I'm	lot	neighborhood	playing
if	lots	neighbors	pretty
*in	*love	never	put
into	make	new	reach
*is	mama	next	read
*it	man	nice	reading
it's	married	night	ready
job	math	no	really
joy	may	not	red
July	*me	now	relatives
just	mean	*of	rich
keep	meeting	off	ride
kind	memories	old	right
*know	met	*on	running
ladies	mind	*one	safe
land	miss	only	said
last	money	open	say
late	more	or	*school
later	morning	other	see
learn	most	our	*she
leave	mother	out	sister
let	mother's	over	sitting
life	mountain	own	skating
*like	move	parents	sky
likes	mrs.	party	small
little	much	*people	*so
live	*my	person	soccer
long	myself	picnic	*some
look	name	plan	someday
looking	need	play	someone
Lord	needs	played	something

sometimes	*they	*was	*would
song	*thing	watch	wouldn't
soon	things	**watching**	write
special	think	water	year
sports	thinking	**way**	years
start	**this**	*we	*you
stay	those	week	your
still	three	weekend	
stop	*time	well	
story	tired	went	
study	*to	were	
summer	**today**	what	
Sunday	**together**	*when	
supper	**told**	where	
swimming	**too**	which	
take	top	**while**	
talk	**trip**	white	
talking	trouble	**who**	
teacher	**true**	**why**	
team	**try**	*will	
tell	**two**	**wish**	
than	until	*with	
thanks	**up**	women	
*that	us	**won't**	
that's	used	words	
*the	**vacation**	**work**	
their	**very**	**working**	
them	wait	**world**	
then	*want	worries	
there	wanted	worry	
these	wants	worst	

APPENDIX B   Alternative Reading Materials

advertisements from newspapers, magazines, and catalogues
airline schedules
bulletin boards
calendars
catalogues
classified sections of magazines, weeklies, and newspapers
comic strips
directions from models, and science experiments
directories
driver's manuals
excerpts from articles, stories, descriptions, and essays
game boxes, directions, and rules
greeting cards
grocery items
headlines
indexes from books or complete volumes
invitations to parties and other events
jackets from books
jokes in newspapers, youth publications, magazines, or books
labels from clothing, food, appliances, or furniture
license plates
letters
lunchroom signs
lyrics of familiar songs
magazines
mail
manuals
maps

menus

movie information

museum brochures

newspapers

neighborhood bulletins

notices

obituaries

office materials

original or creative writings

packages from grocery or department stores

pamphlets

passports

passenger lists from tours, flights, passages, and trips

periodicals

pet materials

picture postcards

plays

posters

price tags

programs

puzzles

questionnaires

railway schedules

recipes and cookbooks

recreation materials

real estate signs

riddles

sales slips, receipts, and contracts

schedules of school events or community happenings

signs

slogans for elections, campaigns, or groups

snack bar posters
speeches
sports materials
tax forms
TV guides
telegrams
theater programs, tickets, and advertisements
thesaurus
tickets
toy wrappings, descriptions, and directions for assembling and
   using
travel brochures
touring itineraries
warranties
weather reports
wedding announcements
wills and testaments
zoo signs

Journal of Reading Article Reference List

Listed here is complete reference information for the *Journal of Reading* articles adapted in this book.

Arthur, Beth M. (1991, May). Working with new ESL students in a junior high school reading class. *Journal of Reading, 34*, 628–631.

Austin-Anglea, Lynne. (1990, December). Word banks for adult literacy. *Journal of Reading, 34*, 300–301.

Best, Pat. (1990, November). Correcting adult students' writing errors. *Journal of Reading, 34*, 222–223.

D'Angelo, Karen. (1983, March). Précis writing: Promoting vocabulary development and comprehension. *Journal of Reading, 26*, 534–539.

Dwyer, Edward J. (1984, December). Developing writing skills through letter writing. *Journal of Reading, 28*, 272–273.

Fellios, Constance Lessaris. (1992, March). Continuing fun with short stories and writing. *Journal of Reading, 35*, 480–481.

Finley, Claudia D., & Seaton, Martha N. (1987, November). Using text patterns and question prediction to study for tests. *Journal of Reading, 31*, 124–132.

Forester, Anne D. (1988, April). Learning to read and write at 26. *Journal of Reading, 31*, 604–613.

Garfield, Sara. (1993, September). Beyond the barriers: Creative writing with adult remedial students. *Journal of Reading, 37*, 55–56.

Goldstein, Bobbye S. (1986, April). Looking at cartoons and comics in a new way. *Journal of Reading, 29*, 657–661.

Haggard, Martha Rapp. (1982, December). The Vocabulary Self-Collection Strategy: An active approach to word learning. *Journal of Reading, 26*, 203–207.

Henk, William A., & Helfeldt, John P. (1987, April). How to develop independence in following written directions. *Journal of Reading, 30*, 602–607.

Hicks, Karen, & Wadlington, Beth. (1994, February). Bigger is better: Shared Book Experience with adults. *Journal of Reading, 37*, 422–423.

Jacobowitz, Tina. (1988, November). Using theory to modify practice: An illustration with SQ3R. *Journal of Reading, 32*, 126–131.

Jeremiah, Milford A. (1988, November). Summaries improve comprehension. *Journal of Reading, 32*, 172–173.

Keefe, Donald, & Meyer, Valerie. (1991, November). Teaching adult new readers the whole language way. *Journal of Reading, 35*, 180–183.

Kossack, Sharon, & Hoffman, Edwina. (1987, November). A picture's worth a thousand words: Comprehension processing via the comics. *Journal of Reading, 31*, 174–176.

Laffey, Donna G., & Laffey, James L. (1986, April). Vocabulary teaching: An investment in literacy. *Journal of Reading, 29*, 650–656.

LaSasso, Carol. (1983, March). Using the *National Enquirer* with unmotivated or language-handicapped readers. *Journal of Reading, 26*, 546–548.

Lee, Nancy G., & Neal, Judith C. (1992, December). Reading Rescue: Intervention for a student "at promise." *Journal of Reading, 36*, 276–282.

Lie, Anita. (1993, May). Paired Storytelling: An integrated approach for EFL students. *Journal of Reading, 36*, 656–658.

Meyer, Valerie. (1987, December). Lingering feelings of failure: An adult student who didn't learn to read. *Journal of Reading, 31*, 218–221.

Meyer, Valerie, Estes, Sharon L., Harris, Valorie K., & Daniels, David M. (1991, September). Case study—Norman: Literate at age 44. *Journal of Reading, 35*, 38–42.

Miller, P.A. (1988, October). Using annual reports for adult literacy improvement. *Journal of Reading, 32*, 25–29.

Moore, David W., & Readence, John E. (1980, April). Processing main ideas through parallel lesson transfer. *Journal of Reading, 23*, 589–593.

Ollmann, Hilda E. (1993, April). How to choose a good book. *Journal of Reading, 36*, 565–567.

Olson, Mary W., Gee, Thomas C., & Forester, Nora. (1989, May). Magazines in the classroom: Beyond recreational reading. *Journal of Reading, 32*, 708–713.

Padak, Gary M., & Padak, Nancy D. (1987, March). Guidelines and a holistic method for adult basic reading programs. *Journal of Reading, 30*, 490–496.

Padak, Nancy D., Davidson, Jane L., & Padak, Gary M. (1990, September). Exploring reading with adult beginning readers. *Journal of Reading, 34*, 26–29.

Perin, Dolores. (1988, October). Schema activation, cooperation, and adult literacy instruction. *Journal of Reading, 32*, 54–62.

Pitts, Murray M. (1983, March). Comprehension monitoring: Definition and practice. *Journal of Reading, 26*, 516–523.

Porter, Dwight. (1990, February). Précis writing in the ESL classroom. *Journal of Reading, 33*, 381.

Pyle, Valerie S. (1990, February). SSRW—Beyond silent reading. *Journal of Reading, 33*, 379–380.

Journal of Reading

Rosow, La Vergne. (1990, December). Consumer advocacy, empowerment, and adult literacy. *Journal of Reading, 34*, 258–262.

Ruddiman, Joan. (1993, February). The Vocab Game: Empowering students through word awareness. *Journal of Reading, 36*, 400–401.

Ryder, Randall James. (1986, October). Teaching vocabulary through external context clues. *Journal of Reading, 30*, 61–65.

Schierloh, Jane McCabe. (1992, May). Using classic novels with adult new readers. *Journal of Reading, 35*, 618–622.

Sellers, Gayla. (1988, October). Vowel-Sound-Stick: Word attack for secondary remedial students. *Journal of Reading, 32*, 42–45.

Sharp, Peggy A. (1991, November). Picture books in the adult literacy curriculum. *Journal of Reading, 35*, 216–219.

Solé, Dorothy. (1990, December). Using student journals in the workplace ESL classroom. *Journal of Reading, 34*, 301.

Spires, Hiller A. (1992, April). Using writing to explore academic self-perceptions. *Journal of Reading, 35*, 582–583.

Stasz, B.B., Schwartz, R.G., & Weeden, J.C. (1991, September). Writing our lives: An adult basic skills program. *Journal of Reading, 35*, 30–33.

Thistlethwaite, Linda L. (1990, May). Critical reading for at-risk students. *Journal of Reading, 33*, 586–593.

Wangberg, E.G., Thompson, B., & Levitov, J.E. (1984, December). First steps toward an adult basic word list. *Journal of Reading, 28*, 244–247.

Wolfe, Ronald, & Lopez, Alice. (1992, December). Structured overviews for teaching science concepts and terms. *Journal of Reading, 36*, 315–317.

Young, Deborah, & Irwin, Martha. (1988, April). Integrating computers into adult literacy programs. *Journal of Reading, 31*, 648–652.